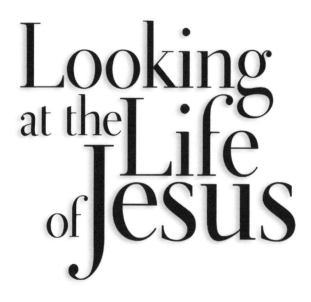

Looking at the Life of Jesus

Rebecca Manley Pippert

InterVarsity Press
Downers Grove, Illinois
Leicester, England

InterVarsity Press
P.O. Box 1400, Downers Grove, IL 60515-1426
World Wide Web: www.ivpress.com
E-mail: mail@ivpress.com

Inter-Varsity Press, England
38 De Montfort Street, Leicester LE1 7GP, England
World Wide Web: www.ivpbooks.com
E-mail: ivp@uccf.org.uk

©2003 by Rebecca Manley Pippert

InterVarsity Press® is the book-publishing division of InterVarsity Christian
Fellowship/USA®, a student movement active on campus at hundreds of
universities, colleges and schools of nursing in the United States of America, and a
member movement of the International Fellowship of Evangelical Students. For
information about local and regional activities, write Public Relations Dept.,
InterVarsity Christian Fellowship/USA, 6400 Schroeder Rd., P.O. Box 7895,
Madison, WI 53707-7895, or visit the IVCF website at <www.ivcf.org>.

Inter-Varsity Press, England, is the book-publishing division of the Universities and
Colleges Christian Fellowship (formerly the Inter-Varsity Fellowship), a student
movement linking Christian Unions in universities and colleges throughout the
United Kingdom and the Republic of Ireland, and a member movement of the
International Fellowship of Evangelical Students. For information about local and
national activities write to UCCF, 38 De Montfort Street, Leicester LE1 7GP.

All Scripture quotations, unless otherwise indicated, are taken from the Holy Bible,
New International Version®. NIV®. Copyright ©1973, 1978, 1984 by
International Bible Society. Used by permission of Zondervan Publishing House. All
rights reserved. Distributed in the U.K. by permission of Hodder and Stoughton Ltd.
All rights reserved. "NIV" is a registered trademark of International Bible Society.
UK trademark number 1448790.

Cover design: Cindy Kiple

Cover and interior image: Philippe Colombi/Getty Images

U.S. ISBN 0-8308-2122-8

U.K. ISBN 0-85111-790-2

Printed in the United States of America ∞

| P | 15 | 14 | 13 | 12 | 11 | 10 | 9 | 8 | 7 | 6 | 5 | 4 | 3 | 2 | 1 |
| Y | 13 | 12 | 11 | 10 | 09 | 08 | 07 | 06 | 05 | 04 | 03 | | | | |

To Ruth Siemens,

My mentor, my friend and

a true hero of the faith,

whose life has shaped not only mine

but countless others around the world.

I dedicate this series to you—

with gratitude beyond expression.

CONTENTS

INTRODUCTION

Socrates said the unexamined life is not worth living. Yet leading an examined life in our unexamining age is quite a challenge. The pressure and pace of life leave little time for reflection—and people are paying a steep price for it. We are left searching for something worth living for and for some way to be at peace with ourselves, to calm the inner conflicts and feelings of personal inadequacy that make us so dissatisfied with ourselves. As part of our search for meaning and peace, growing numbers of us are seeing therapists, spending exorbitant sums on plastic surgery and relentlessly pursuing wealth and prestige, yet we still wind up feeling empty.

How can we discover and live with a deeper sense of life's meaning? Jesus said, "Come to me, all you who are weary and burdened, and I will give you rest" (Matthew 11:28). It is a remarkable statement made by a remarkable man. Jesus forgave sins and claimed to have special insight into who God is. He also claimed that he had always existed and that one day he would return at the end of time. He not only talked as if he was God, he boldly proclaimed, "I am the resurrection and the life. . . . Whoever lives and believes in me will never die" (John 11:25-26). Jesus insisted that if we desire to find joy, peace and inner transformation, then he's our man. So if his claims are true, if he really is who he says he is, then according to Jesus, to miss him would be to miss life itself.

How do we study the life of Jesus, especially if we do not know what we believe? Jesus said it best when he told his disciples to simply "come and see." As you read different Bible passages and observe Jesus in all kinds of situations, you will likely discover, as I did, that Jesus is quite different from what you thought.

I vividly remember the first time I read the Gospel of John as an agnostic seeker. My impression of Jesus was that he was sincere and kind, wearing an other-worldly, beatific smile. Then I started reading the Bible. I was not prepared for what I discovered. Here was a man who claimed to be the Messiah, the Prince of Peace, yet he threw furniture down the front steps of the Temple. The religious accused him of being a drunk, a glutton and having terrible taste in friends. He claimed to be the Son of God, yet one of the chief complaints against him was that he wasn't religious enough! This was not the kind of Jesus I had expected to encounter.

Maybe you're at the same place I was, and you've never read the Bible before. Or perhaps you vaguely remember Bible stories from your childhood but you've never looked at the life of Christ with a critical, adult mind. Whatever your story, one thing is certain: it's impossible to make an informed decision without first knowing the facts. I wrote this guide for anyone who is genuinely seeking, who has honest questions and who wants to take a fresh look at the real Jesus

Using This Discussion Guide

Since my own journey began in skepticism, where I was encouraged to ask questions and never asked to adopt belief blindly, I have chosen a similar approach in these Bible discussions. It is not necessary that you believe in Jesus or accept the Bible as "divinely inspired" in order to use this guide. Rather, come to the accounts of Jesus as you would to any sound history, with an open mind and heart to see what you find.

This guide is based on the Gospel of John, which most scholars conclude was written by John, one of the twelve disciples of Jesus. When John sat down to write his Gospel, there were already three other gospels in existence: Matthew, Mark and Luke. The best evidence points to a composition date around A.D. 90, and he most likely wrote it from Ephesus, which was located in what is modern-day Turkey. Throughout the Gospel, John never mentions himself by name, instead referring to himself simply as "the disciple whom Jesus loved."

John offers a fascinating perspective on the life of Jesus because he was an eyewitness to most of the events he writes about. He followed Jesus from the very beginning of his ministry, and he was one of the inner circle of Jesus' three closest friends. When Jesus was on the cross, it was John who he entrusted to care for his mother.

This guide is written to encourage give-and-take group discussion led by a moderator. The open-style discussion challenges you as participants to wrestle with the text yourselves and to reach your own conclusions. Don't feel intimidated if this is your first time reading the Bible; that means your contributions to group discussions will be fresh and stimulating. Remember, there is no homework. If you want to answer the questions ahead of time go right ahead (space is provided for writing answers to each question). If you are able to read the passage ahead of time, then do so. But it's also fine to simply show up each week at your study without having prepared ahead of time.

How do we use these studies? The "Discussion Starter" question is simply meant to kick off the discussion for a few minutes. The section on historical context is intended to be read aloud. Its purpose is to provide some historical or cultural background. The "Discovering Jesus" section contains questions that make us engage the text in order to understand its meaning. The "Live What You Learn" question is to help us *apply* the truth we've studied to our everyday lives. The sidebar quotes are simply for your enjoyment!

The guide includes seven stories from the life of Jesus so that you may begin to get a sense of his person, his teaching, his actions and his claims. John's deepest desire in writing this book was "that you may believe that Jesus is the Christ, the Son of God" (John 20:31). For John was convinced, as I now am, that it is through faith in Jesus that we become fully alive and truly human.

ONE

Profits or Prophets
in the Church?

Discussion Starter

What are common complaints people have against organized religious institutions such as the church?

Historical Context

We are about to read a story of how Jesus responded to the hypocrisy and greed of some of the religious leaders of his day. If you believe that "gentle Jesus meek and mild" is an accurate historical portrayal of Jesus, then you may be in for a surprise.

This is Jesus' first official public appearance in Jerusalem: the religious, political, educational and cultural capital of the Jews. In our age of extreme political correctness, it is astonishing to see Jesus break every possible rule of perceived correctness. The occasion was the great annual celebration of the Passover, when all good Jews made the pilgrimage to the Holy City to observe commemoration of God's mighty, historical rescue of his people from Egyptian slavery. The pilgrims came for two primary reasons—(1) to worship God (by making animal sacrifices) and (2) to pray.

◆ Discovering Jesus

Read John 2:13-25.

1. Imagine the thousands of pilgrims crowding the streets and courtyards of the great temple. What can you hear? see? smell?

   What is the mood of the people?

2. What provoked Jesus' anger?

3. What suggests that this wasn't an impulsive act of simply losing his temper (v. 15)?

4. There were other people who undoubtedly saw the scandal of what was happening in the temple precincts. Why was Jesus the only one who was so outraged?

What is significant about how Jesus speaks of God in verse 16?

5. Verse 17 refers to Psalm 69:9. How did this Old Testament verse help clarify for the disciples why Jesus responded so passionately?

Picture the scene: A hitherto unknown man walks into the magnificent temple precincts. In the intimidating presence of the priests of the temple, he not only turns tables upside down but directly challenges them, saying, "How dare you turn my Father's house into a market?"

6. Why do you think these proud religious leaders did not stop this peasant carpenter from the back-

woods of Nazareth who was challenging their authority?

7. How did Jesus respond to the temple authorities' demands for credentials (vv. 18-20)?

8. What connection does Jesus' answer have with their request (v. 19)?

9. In what tone of voice do you suppose verse 20 was spoken?

10. The disciples didn't immediately grasp what Jesus was talking about when he said, "Destroy this temple, and I will raise it again in three days." But after Jesus' death this incident came to the minds of the

disciples and it encouraged them. Why?

11. If people were believing in Jesus because of the miraculous signs, why didn't Jesus "entrust himself to them" (vv. 23-25)?

12. Contrast the Pharisees' attitude and Jesus' attitude toward God, common people and religious hyprocisy.

▶ Live What You Learn

13. What would you say to a person who is fed up with religious hypocrisy regarding what you have learned about Jesus thus far?

"I was given the impression that Jesus was a gentle creature. . . . Then I looked at the New Testament. There I found an account, not in the least of a person with his hair parted in the middle or his hands clasped in appeal, but an extraordinary being with lips of thunder and acts of lurid decision, casting out devils, passing with the wild secrecy of the wind. . . . He flung furniture down the front steps of the Temple and asked men how they expected to escape the damnation of Hell. He said such weak and innocuous things as 'I've come to set the earth on fire.' The diction used about Christ has been, perhaps wisely, sweet and submissive. But the diction used by Christ is quite curiously gigatesque, it is full of camels leaping through needles and mountains hurled into the sea."

G. K. CHESTERTON, *ORTHODOXY*

G. K. Chesterton (1874-1936) was a journalist, an essayist, a humorist and one of the most brilliant defenders of the Christian faith in the twentieth century. In an age of pessimism and doubt he powerfully defended the faith in debates with such renowned figures as George Bernard Shaw. A prolific author, his most famous books are Orthodoxy *and the Father Brown detective stories. Here we read his surprise at having first encountered the Jesus described in the Bible.*

Two

Water for a Dry Soul

Discussion Starter

Why do unchurched people sometimes feel uncomfortable around religious people?

Historical Context

We are about to read a story in which Jesus does the inconceivable. In his culture it was considered the height of impropriety for a religious man to talk with a woman; but to speak to a woman of low moral standing was unheard of. Consider these Rabbinic warnings taught by the Jewish leaders of Jesus' day: "One should not talk with a woman on the street, not even with his own wife, and certainly not with someone else's wife, because of the gossip of men." "It is forbidden to give a woman any greeting."

Besides ignoring these social prejudices, Jesus overlooked the deep racial and religious prejudice that Jews felt towards Samaritans. The orthodox Jews of Jesus' day looked on the Samaritans as a corrupt race because their Gentile ancestors had intermarried with Jews. The Jews also despised the Samaritans for having a *mixed religion*, which accepted pagan idolatry with elements of the Hebrew faith. The feeling was mutual; the Samaritans often refused lodging to Jews passing though their territory, so Jews often traveled to the east side of the Jordan River to avoid Samaria. The bitterness between Jews and Samaritans was at its height in Jesus' day.

◆ Discovering Jesus

Read John 4:4-15.

1. Why have Jesus and his disciples stopped at Sychar? Tell everything you can about Jesus' physical and mental state (vv. 7-8).

2. Consider the hot Middle East climate. Why do you think the woman is drawing water at midday?

3. Why is the woman initially shocked at Jesus' request?

4. We can only imagine how this woman was used to

being treated by men. Jesus begins his conversation with this woman by sharing his personal need rather than first addressing her problem. What does this reveal about Jesus' understanding of human nature and of this woman in particular?

5. Describe the woman's reaction to Jesus' offer in verses 11-12. Do you think she understands what Jesus is offering?

6. What does Jesus say about this "living water" that makes it so appealing to her (vv. 13-14)?

Read John 4:16-30.

7. This is a crucial point in the conversation. Just when the woman asks to receive this living water, Jesus suddenly delves into her personal life and asks her to go call her husband. Why?

8. How does she respond to Jesus' question with only a half-truth?

9. Jesus affirms her for answering honestly, but why do you think he brings up her list of past marriages and present problematic relationship (vv. 16-18)?

10. No doubt stunned by Jesus' knowledge of her personal life, she changes the subject to the controversy over the proper place of worship (vv. 19-20). What does Jesus teach about true worship (vv. 22-24)?

11. Note the disciples' reaction upon returning to the scene. How do you think the woman felt knowing that Jesus didn't ignore her when they arrived (v. 27)?

12. What is the significance of her leaving her water jug (vv. 28-30)?

Read John 4:39-42.

13. Describe the woman's message to the townspeople and their response (vv. 39-42).

14. What was it about her encounter with Jesus that freed her to be so transparent about her life?

Live What You Learn

15. The religious and respectable people of Jesus' day would have regarded this woman as a lost cause. Even his own disciples were shocked that Jesus was speaking to her. What did Jesus see in her and her predicament (her "thirst") that apparently no one else did?

16. How does it affect your attitude to others, or even to yourself, to know that Jesus considers no one a lost cause?

"I may, I suppose, regard myself, or pass for being, a relatively successful man. People occasionally stare at me in the streets—that's fame. I can fairly easily earn enough to qualify for admission to the higher slopes of the Inland Revenue [the equivalent of the Internal Revenue Service]—that's success. Furnished with money and a little of success even the elderly, if they care to, may partake of trendy diversions—that's pleasure. It might even happen once in a while that something I said or wrote was sufficiently heeded for me to persuade myself that it represented a significant impact of our time—that's fulfillment. Yet I say to you, and I beg you to believe me, multiply these tiny triumphs by a million, add them all together, and they are nothing—less than nothing, a positive impediment—measured against one draught of that living water Christ offers to the spiritually thirsty, irrespective of who or what they are."

MALCOLM MUGGERIDGE,
AS CITED IN J. GLADSTONE, *LIVING WITH STYLE*

Malcolm Muggeridge (1903-1990), an English journalist and former editor of Punch *magazine, was known for his great satiric wit and devastating political and social critiques. A celebrated and outspoken skeptic of the Christian faith, his conversion to Christianity in his mid-life was an astonishment to his public and to himself! Read about his faith journey in* Chronicles of Wasted Years *or the Christian thinkers who most inspired him in his book* A Third Testament. *It was Muggeridge who is credited for introducing Mother Teresa to the world stage in his book* Something Beautiful for God.

THREE

Soul Food

Discussion Starter

Sooner or later most of us face an impossible situation that leaves us feeling inadequate. Do you think seeing our inadequacies is helpful or harmful? What types of things do people often turn to for help?

Historical Context

In the passage we are reading today Jesus' disciples come up against the reality of their own inadequacies in seemingly impossible situations.

This event takes place around the end of Jesus' second year of ministry. A year has passed since Jesus turned the tables over in the Jerusalem temple (John 2). During this time Jesus has ministered largely in and around Galilee.

The Galileans were peasants who lived close to the soil and worked hard for their wages. They were concerned with practical matters such as food and their livelihood, not like the more sophisticated Jerusalem crowd that Jesus had previously encountered whose concerns were more theoretical and theological.

In Mark 6:30-31 we learn that the disciples have just returned from a highly successful preaching tour and they need rest. To get privacy Jesus takes his disciples to the hills to the east of the sea of Galilee, also known as the Golan Heights. But the crowd, who has heard of Jesus' miracles among the sick, gets wind of Jesus' wherabouts and follows him round the lake.

◆ Discovering Jesus

Read John 6:1-15.

1. From the information in verses 2-5, describe the situation. (Why had the crowd followed Jesus? What is Jesus doing? What are the people doing?)

2. If Jesus knew what he was going to do (v. 6) why did he ask his disciples how they could feed the crowd?

3. How did Philip, who was from nearby Bethsaida and thus knew the territory well, respond to Jesus' question (vv. 5-7)?

Why do you think Jesus was unperturbed by the offering of such a measly resource for such a vast crowd?

4. How do you think the disciples and the people sitting on the grass might have felt as they heard Jesus giving thanks for the food (vv. 10-11)?

5. How do you think the disciples felt as they collected up the pieces left over (vv. 12-13)?

6. Since it is almost time for the Passover feast, which celebrates when God through Moses fed his people supernaturally with manna from heaven, the crowd concludes this is the prophet whom Moses had said would come. What was Jesus' response to the people saying that he would become a political king (vv. 14-15)?

7. In verses 3 and 15 we see Jesus withdraw from the people. Why do you think he does this?

Read John 6:25-35.

8. How did Jesus assess the crowd's motive in seaching for him, and what is their main error (vv. 25-27)?

9. As long as people came to Jesus seeking only temporal things (free food and a political Messiah who will rid them of Roman rule), Jesus knew their deepest needs would go unmet. What does Jesus want them to focus on (vv. 27, 29)?

10. What do you think Jesus meant when he called himself the Bread of Life?

How will this satisfy their deepest needs (vv. 35)?

Live What You Learn

11. The crowd was so obsessed with getting their physical needs met that they failed to understand Jesus' greater offer to meet their deepest needs and yearnings. How can our immediate needs or worries blind us from seeing our deeper spiritual needs?

12. How can our trials bring us closer to God?

*"You promised them the Bread of Heaven, but I re-
peat again, can it compare with earthly bread in the
eyes of the weak, ever sinful and ever ignoble race?
. . . Yet in this question lies hidden the great secret
of this world. Choosing [Christ's] 'bread,' you would
have satisfied the universal and everlasting craving
of humanity—to find someone to worship. So long
as man remains free he strives for nothing so inces-
santly and so painfully as to find someone to worship. . . . For the secret of man's being is not only to
live but to have something to live for. Without a
clear conception of the object of life, man would not
consent to go on living and would rather destroy
himself than remain on earth, though he had bread
in abundance."*

FYODOR DOSTOYEVSKY, *THE BROTHERS KARAMAZOV*

---

*Dostoyevsky (1821-1881) was a Russian novelist whose
brilliance was matched by a life full of contradictions and
paradoxes. He was frequently in debt, subject to epileptic
seizures, and plagued by tragedy and loss. Yet he slowly
came to the conclusion that only faith in God could make life
meaningful and lift humankind from its tragic and fallen
condition. This excerpt is from the legendary chapter "The
Grand Inquisitor" in* The Brothers Karamazov. *Ivan, an
intellectual atheist, rigorously defends his doubts and
rejection of God to his novice monk brother, Alyosha, through
a prose poem he has written in which the Grand Inquisitor
ridicules the Divine Visitor. Ironically his very attack against
Christ still provides arguments for faith.*

Four

I Once Was Blind . . .

> ## Discussion Starter

What fears do you have about what others might think if they discover you are a spiritual seeker?

Historical Context

We are about to read a passage in which a genuine seeker comes to believe in Jesus and then experiences repercussions and even persecution for his faith. This story is about a man who gets caught in the political meat grinder of religious politics. He reminds us of how important it is to stay open to the truth and to not allow any preconceived views or agendas to keep us from experiencing God's truth.

The Jewish rabbis of Jesus' day espoused the belief that people suffered disabilities because of their sin or the sin of their parents. Eastern religion also teaches that our sins in this life will come and haunt us in the next life. Jesus defies the notion that our "karma" or our present suffering can always be blamed on our sin or that of others. Instead Jesus teaches and performs a miracle that sets a man free from decades of shame and suffering.

◆ Discovering Jesus

Read John 9:1-5.

1. Based on the question the disciples ask Jesus (v. 2), what did they believe was the cause of this man's suffering?

   How does Jesus' response to the disciples' question give suffering people hope (v. 3)?

2. In verse 5 Jesus claims to be the light of the world. How does he confirm that spiritual claim?

Read John 9:6-13.

3. Imagine you are the blind beggar. We are told that a blind person has exquisite senses in other areas.

I Once Was Blind . . .

What would he have heard, felt or sensed from Jesus' interaction with him?

4. Jesus healed people in widely different ways. Why do you think Jesus goes through the process of making mud and instructs the man to go wash, instead of healing him instantly?

5. Describe what it would have been like for the healed man to see vivid colors and people's expressions for the first time.

How did the people who knew him respond (vv. 8-13)?

Read John 9:14-34.

6. Why do the Pharisees object to this miracle (vv. 16, 22, 24, 29)?

7. Still skeptical, the Pharisees send for the man's parents (v. 18). Why were the blind man's parents so cautious as they answered their questions (vv. 18-23)?

8. In the Pharisees' second interview with this healed man, what points did he make in answer to their unreasonable objections (vv. 30-33)?

9. How do the Pharisee react when they are at a loss to prove the miracle didn't occur (vv. 28-34)?

Read John 9:35-41.

10. For what two reasons did Jesus seek out the healed man the second time (v. 35)?

11. The man worships Jesus in verse 38. How would you describe the range of emotions this man has experienced throughout the events of this story?

12. What kept the religious leaders from seeing the truth?

 **Live What You Learn**

13. We learn from this man's story that faith is a process. How have your ideas about God changed over the years and why?

14. The shame and suffering of this man's life was clearly alleviated by Jesus' healing. Yet there were serious repercussions for him in coming to believe in Jesus. How can a full commitment to faith in Christ cause tensions in a person's life even today?

"Amazing grace! how sweet the sound
that saved a wretch like me!
I once was lost but now am found,
Was blind, but now I see.

'Twas grace that taught my heart to fear,
And grace my fears relieved,
How precious did that grace appear
The hour I first believed."

JOHN NEWTON, "AMAZING GRACE"

John Newton (1725-1807), the author of this beloved hymn, was a British sailor whose life of debauchery and sin took him to the western coast of Africa, where he eventually got involved in the African slave trade. His dramatic conversion during a violent storm in the North Atlantic changed his life forever. He sought orders to become an Anglican clergyman, served as spiritual counselor to influential leaders and wrote hundreds of hymns, including "Amazing Grace." In his later years he played a leading role in Wilberforce's political campaign against slave trading.

FIVE

Eternal Life

> ## Discussion Starter

What are some of your honest feelings and fears about death—especially when a family member or a friend dies?

> ## Historical Context

We are about to read a story in which a beloved friend of Jesus dies. You may be surprised, even shocked by Jesus' reactions and responses, but it gives us an opportunity to learn more about what Jesus was like and what he thought about death.

When Jesus was last in Jerusalem, the controversy and attacks against him were increasingly intense. The Jews were divided: some believed in him, some said he was demon-possessed, others dismissed him as a lunatic, still others wondered how an evil man could be used of God to perform miracles. However, at the Feast of Dedication things reached a fever-pitch when Jesus claimed equality with God (10:30), which prompted his antagonists to pick up stones to kill him (stoning was the accepted punishment for blasphemy; see John 10:33). It was dangerous for Jesus to stay in Jerusalem, and since he knew it wasn't yet his time to die, he left temporarily and began ministering across the Jordan river.

However, while he was there he received an urgent request for help. His dear friend Lazarus, the brother of Mary and Martha, was very sick. These friends lived in Bethany, a few miles southeast from Jerusalem, where Jesus had been a frequent guest in their home. Lazarus and his sisters felt great affection for Jesus and he for them.

◆ Discovering Jesus

Read John 11:1-16.

1. What was Jesus' immediate response when he heard the news about Lazarus (vv. 4-6)?

2. The text makes it clear that Jesus loves Lazarus, yet he deliberately delays in coming. Jesus would have wanted to go immediately, but what did he know that enabled him to wait (vv. 4, 15)?

Why is it important that Lazarus' death be firmly established if Jesus' goal was to be accomplished?

3. Why were the disciples shocked at Jesus' decision to go to Judea (v. 8)?

4. What reason did Jesus give for going (vv. 9-15)?

5. How would you characterize Thomas's response (v. 16)?

Read John 11:17-27.

6. Describe the scene as Jesus approached the home of Martha and Mary (vv. 17-19).

7. What elements of doubt and faith do you see in Martha's response to Jesus (vv. 20-22, 24, 27)?

8. In verse 24 Martha makes the statement, "I know he will rise again in the resurrection at the last day." But what extraordinary claim does Jesus make that takes her faith even further (vv. 25-26)?

Read John 11:28-44.

9. How does John carefully describe the various stages of Jesus' response to the grief and anguish of Mary and those who came with her (vv. 33, 35, 38)?

10. The words John uses to describe Jesus' response in verse 38, "deeply moved," imply not simply intense grief but deep anger—like a snorting horse on its hind legs. Why do you think Jesus responds to Lazarus' death, and the enormous grief it caused Mary and Martha, not only with compassionate grief but with outrage?

11. What does Jesus say, through his words and prayer, was the purpose of this event (vv. 40, 42)?

12. Describe the extraordinary event that took place at Jesus' command.

What would it have been like to witness the events of verses 43-44?

Live What You Learn

13. What does this story teach us about our frustration when God seems to delay in answering our prayers?

14. The natural human yearning is that we and those we love should never die. Does the miracle of Lazarus and Jesus' words to Martha, "Whoever lives and believes in me will never die" (v. 26), give you hope? Why or why not?

"Creatures are not born with desires unless satisfaction for those desires exists. A baby feels hunger: well, there is such a thing as food. A duckling wants to swim: well, there is such a thing as water. If I find in myself a desire which no experience in this world can satisfy, the most probable explanation is that I was made for another world. I must keep alive in myself the desire for my true country, which I shall not find till after death: I must never let it get snowed under or turned aside; I must make it the main object of life to press on to that other country and to help others to do the same."

C. S. LEWIS, *MERE CHRISTIANITY*

C. S. Lewis (1898-1963) was a scholar and writer who taught English language and literature at Oxford University in England. Well into his adult life he was a staunch atheist. After his astonishing conversion to Christianity (documented in his book Surprised by Joy)*, he eventually went on to become the bestselling Christian author of all time. For a brilliant and lucid explanation of the Christian faith read* Mere Christianity; *for a look at the nature of evil read* The Screwtape Letters.

Six

Death Isn't the Last Word

Discussion Starter

In the 1900s it was widely believed that human nature was fundamentally good and that evil was largely caused by ignorance and bad housing, and that education and social reform would enable us to live together in happiness and good will. What evidence do you see that this was unrealistic?

Historical Context

Christianity begins with the assumption that human beings are in trouble and need rescuing and that God has taken the initiative in sending Jesus Christ to deliver them from their dilemma. What follows is the unfolding of God's rescue mission.

The night before this passage begins, the Roman guards (with the aid of Judas, one of the disciples) arrested Jesus in the Garden of Gethsemane. Next they took Jesus to Annas, a former high priest, who questioned Jesus in an attempt to get evidence to convict him of blasphemy. Then Jesus was sent to the home of Caiaphas, the current high priest, with Peter and most likely John observing from a distance. During the night the Jewish council determined that Jesus should die for blasphemy (Luke 22:63-71), but before the Roman authorities they would falsely charge Jesus with treason in order to obtain the death penalty. (Under Roman rule the Jews had no authority to carry out a death penalty.) Upon completing their mock trial in the very early morning, the Jewish leaders took Jesus to the palace of the Roman governor, Pilate.

Pilate interrogates Jesus and finds him innocent. But the Jewish leaders insist that Jesus be crucified. Next follows a series of compromises on Pilate's part finally leading to his acquiescence to their wishes.

◆ Discovering Jesus

Read John 19:1-16.

1. What verses in this text reveal Pilate's opinion of Jesus (vv. 4, 6, 12)?

2. It was routine treatment to flog a prisoner found guilty. Why does Pilate have Jesus flogged?

3. When the real basis of the Jews' accusation against

Jesus is laid bare, how does it increase Pilate's fear (v. 7)?

4. What is Pilate really asking in verse 9, and why does Jesus not answer?

5. How does Jesus respond to Pilate's claim that he is under Pilate's power (vv. 10-11)?

6. Despite Pilate's firm intention to set Jesus free, what trap did the Jewish leaders use to coerce him to pronounce the death penalty on a man he knew was innocent (vv. 12-15)?

Read John 19:17-27.

7. Recognizing that this is a compressed narrative (each Gospel adds various details), think back on the events of Jesus' last twenty-four hours and describe his physical condition when he is carrying his cross.

8. Why did the Jews object to Pilate's title above Jesus' cross (vv. 19-21)?

9. How was the Old Testament prophecy of Psalm 22:18 fulfilled at the cross (vv. 23-24)?

10. What wonderful provision does Jesus make for his mother before he dies (vv. 26-27)?

Read John 19:28-37.

11. What does Jesus mean by the words "It is finished" (v. 30)?

12. To be absolutely certain that Jesus had died, one soldier pierced his side with a spear. What was the significance of water coming out of the wound as well as blood (vv. 32-34)?

13. What spiritual significance does the author John make about Jesus' death (vv. 35-37)?

◆ Live What You Learn

14. The presence of God in our suffering is one of the supreme distinctives of the Christian faith. The Bible tells us we have a God who enters into our sufferings and shares them with us because he understands from personal experience. What are different ways in which Jesus suffered, and how does that give us courage and hope in our own lives?

15. John 19 reports the event of the cross, but to understand the meaning of the cross, we need to look at other passages of Scripture. Let's hear what the Scriptures say about the heart of sin and why the cross was necessary. Let each member who has a Bible study guide read one verse without comment.

You are a man and not a god,
   though you think you are as wise as a god.
(Ezekiel 28:2)

He was despised and rejected by men,
   a man of sorrows, and familiar with suffering. . . .

But he was pierced for our transgressions,
    he was crushed for our iniquities;
the punishment that brought us peace was upon him,
    and by his wounds we are healed.
We all, like sheep, have gone astray,
    each of us has turned to his own way;
and the LORD has laid on him
    the iniquity of us all. (Isaiah 53:3, 5-6)

"He committed no sin, and no deceit was found in his mouth." When they hurled their insults at him, he did not retaliate; when he suffered he made no threats. Instead, he entrusted himself to him who judges justly. He himself bore our sins in his body on the tree, so that we might die to sins and live for righteousness; by his wounds you have been healed. For you were like sheep going astray, but now you have returned to the Shepherd and Overseer of your souls. (1 Peter 2:22-25).

God made him who had no sin to be sin for us, so that in Him we might become the righteousness of God. (2 Corinthians 5:21)

But God demonstrates his own love for us in this: While we were still sinners, Christ died for us. (Romans 5:8)

"When a man is getting better he understands more and more clearly that evil is still left in him. When a man is getting worse, he understands his badness less and less. A moderately bad man knows he is not very good; a thoroughly bad man thinks he is all right."
C. S. Lewis

"For the essence of sin is man substituting himself for God, while the essence of salvation is God substituting himself for man."
John Stott

SEVEN

The End of Doubt

◇ Discussion Starter

Imagine yourself as one of Jesus' disciples who has followed him faithfully and then just witnessed his crucifixion and burial. What do you feel? What questions would you ask?

◆ Historical Context

Those days following the crucifixion were undoubtedly the worst days of the disciples' lives. On the one hand, the Jewish leaders and Roman government were turning Jerusalem upside down to find his corpse. That was all they needed to prove it was a hoax. Yet the body was never discovered. On the other hand, the disciples were filled with despair and unanswered questions. Surely they wondered why Jesus did not escape when the guards came to arrest him in Gethsemane. Why did Jesus deliberately give himself over to them? Why did he insist on dying? None of it made any sense.

When Jesus died, it seemed his cause had suffered permanent defeat. His closest followers were bewildered and grief-stricken. Many had made great sacrifices to follow him. They believed he was the promised Messiah just as he had said he was. He had performed supernatural acts, healed the blind and sick, even raised Lazarus from dead, but now he himself was dead. Two of the Jewish religious leaders, members of the ruling counsel and secret believers in Christ, asked Pilate for Jesus' body and put him in a tomb. Jesus' friends also brought spices for the embalming. Yards of cloth were wrapped around the body with many pounds of spices laid in between layers. A very heavy stone (that would have required many men to remove) was rolled to cover the door. Expert soldiers (similar to our Green Beret) were ordered to guard the tomb.

Discovering Jesus

Read John 20:1-10.

1   Set the scene in verses 1-2. (What did Mary Magdalene see? How do you think she felt? What does she think has happened?)

2.   What is the reaction of Peter and John in verses 3-8?

3.   How did they know something supernatural had transpired concerning Jesus?

What was it that they still didn't understand (v. 9)?

Read John 20:11-18.

4. Describe Mary's state of mind from verses 11-14.

5. Why does Mary at first fail to recognize Jesus?

6. After she does recognize Jesus, what stands out to you about their encounter?

7. Why does Jesus tell Mary not to hold on to him (v. 17)? What is the significance of Jesus' saying to Mary, "*my* Father and *your* Father" (v. 17, italics added)?

8. What is significant in Jesus revealing his risen presence to Mary first?

Read John 20:19-29.

9. What do you think was the emotional state of the disciples as they hid behind closed doors (v. 19)?

Why do the disciples think they are seeing a ghost?

What does Jesus mean when he says twice, "Peace be with you"?

10. Why does Jesus show them his hands and side?

11. Why does Thomas have a problem believing the disciples' story (vv. 24-25)?

12. Why does Jesus speak to Thomas in the way that he does?

13. What exactly does Thomas come to believe about Jesus (v. 28)?

14. We have seen two kinds of doubt in the Gospel of John: first, the doubt of closed unbelief that says, "My mind is made up don't confuse me with the facts"; second, the doubt that would like to believe but needs more evidence. Which kind of doubt did Thomas have?

 Live What You Learn

15. How would you characterize your own state of doubt or belief?

16. Read verse 31. Why does John say he has written this Gospel?

What does John mention are the two distinguishing characteristics of a true follower of Christ?

"When I go down to the grave, I can say like so many others that I have finished my day's work: but I cannot say that I have finished my life. Another day's work will begin the next morning. The tomb is not a blind alley—it is a thoroughfare. It closes with the twilight to open with the dawn."

VICTOR HUGO

Victor Hugo (1802-1885) was a French nineteenth century novelist, poet, playwright and leader of the Romantic movement. Hugo's two best-known novels are The Hunchback of Notre Dame and Les Misérables. Hugo was celebrated as a great humanitarian, but the death of his daughter, Leopoldine, in his mid-life caused a profound spiritual crisis that led him to explore spiritual issues. His "Last Will and Testament" contains the clearest declaration of his religious beliefs. In his will, Hugo doesn't describe himself in othodox Christian terms but more as a Christian mystic. Yet few writers have captured the Christian understanding of grace more powerfully than Hugo's character Jan Val Jean in Les Misérables.

LEADER'S NOTES

Here's a little background on how the studies are put together and how to use each component.

Discussion Starter: Use this as an ice breaker to help people feel comfortable. The question addresses everyday concerns as well as an issue that relates to the biblical text. Why do we ask a general question first? People often feel intimidated about reading the Bible. They are afraid their lack of Bible knowledge will show, or they feel hesitant to ask or give an honest response. But if *you* are relaxed and begin the study each week with a provocative question, it will lighten the atmosphere and make the participants feel at ease. Don't spend more then three minutes on the opening question. After discussing the question, there are several sentences you may read that will lead you into the "Historical Context" section.

Historical Context: This gives the participants some historical or cultural background in order to better understand the passage. Sometimes it merely explains what has happened in previous chapters. You may summarize the information or read it aloud while they read along with you (the participants each have a guide). Remember, our role as leaders is not to be a "sage on the stage—but a guide on the side."

Discovering Jesus: These are questions that follow the inductive method. This is an approach that helps them discover, understand and correlate the facts in the text and discover for themselves what the Scripture is saying. One distinctive of a seeker Bible discussion is that the questions do not assume faith on the part of the participant. However, the questions engage the reader to look carefully at the text in order to understand its meaning.

Live What You Learn: These are the application questions. You will notice that as each week progresses the questions become a bit more focused and direct. Try to get through the passage so there's enough time to ask the application question. The more you get everyone participating in the conversation the better. Remember, however, to set the time for your study and stick to it. I would recommend no longer than sixty minutes.

Sidebar Quotes: I have tried to create a format that stimulates and educates people's interest in faith. Thus these quotes not only relate to the text you are studying, but they come from Christian thinkers, many of whom came to faith in their adult lives. Both the quotes and the biographical information are intended to provide insight from thought-provoking Christian thinkers. I didn't intend the quotes to be read aloud. They're just there for interest.

Leader's Notes: This is background data to help you as you prepare the study.

Reading the Text: Should you read the entire passage first or read by sections and ask questions that pertain to each section? That depends on how long the passage is. For example, in John 2, I would suggest you read the whole passage first as it is fairly short. But when a passage is lengthy I would suggest you read it by sections. Also, ask if anyone would like to read, but don't call on someone to read. If no one offers to read then ask your coleader or read it yourself.

What to Do at Your First Study

There are two ways to start a study. One way is to have an introductory meeting. Keep it fun and offer light refreshments and introduce everyone to each other. Then explain your purpose in gathering and select a time to gather that works for everyone. Then hand out the studies and ask them to read the passage ahead of time if they wish. But assure them that "homework" isn't required. If they want to answer the questions in the guide they may; reading the text ahead of time will be helpful. But if they don't have time to do either, that's okay. You don't want them to stay away if they haven't read the passage, especially since you'll be reading it when you meet. Also, discover if everyone has a Bible, and if they don't you can suggest a particular translation. I suggest RSV and NIV.

The other approach is to figure out through conversations which time seems to work for everyone and invite them to come. At the first meeting be sure you have extra Bibles. No one will have read the passage but that's OK. Before you study the passage, be sure to review the purpose for gathering and go over a few of the ground rules. Then after the study you may hand out the Bible study guide and tell them which passage you'll be reading for next time.

Whichever way you choose, here are things to cover in the first meeting:

1. Review the purpose for gathering (pp. 8-9).

2. Go over a few ground rules for discussion (p. 10).

3. Explain a few things about the Bible and John in particular (pp. 9-10).

4. Be sure everyone has a Bible.

STUDY ONE. JOHN 2:13-25.
Profits or Prophets in the Church?

Question 1

This was the temple that Zerubbabel had built five hundred years earlier. But Herod the Great had begun remodeling forty-six years prior to this incident to make it larger and more beautiful. The project still wasn't complete but the temple was a magnificent structure, able to be seen from miles away. Part of the exterior was gold and from a distance it seemed to glow. There were three parts: the outer court, the holy court (where no poor or maimed people or Gentiles could enter) and the Holy of Holies (where God symbolically dwelled and where once a year the High Priest alone could enter to make atonement for the people). The pilgrims would have been buying their animals for sacrifice in the outer courts of the outer temple (the court of the Gentiles) but not in the holy court. When the pilgrims came they created crude shelters to live in for the eight days of celebration. There would be pilgrims from every country in the temple at that time, plus the priests and the temple police. One would have heard numerous languages and seen people dressed in different garbs.

Question 2

At Passover, animals were sacrificed. Pilgrims purchased animals in the temple so they could offer them as sacrifice. Only temple coins could be used, so Greek, Roman and other coinage had to be exchanged. However the priests charged exorbitant rates for their money exchange. That is, the high priesthood had an extortion racket! The whole system was commercialized, worshipers from abroad were cheated by excessive rates, and they charged huge fees for the cost of animals. The priests made financial gain through this, especially the high priest. The poor people who had come to sincerely worship deeply resented it.

Furthermore, the high priests in Jesus' day were not the descendants of Levi and Aaron, as the Bible required. The priesthood was controlled by a single wealthy family who had bought the privilege from Rome.

Jesus objected not only to the dishonesty but also to

the business conducted on the temple precincts. The temple was the ceremonial place of God's dwelling, and it was to be treated as holy and as a place for prayer—certainly not a place to rip off economically poor pilgrims.

Question 3

The fact that Jesus *made* a cord suggests that this took some time and was a deliberate, intentional act. Jesus didn't simply lose his temper. Consider how long it would take and where he would get the materials. This wasn't a case of uncontrolled rage but righteous indignation at their flagrant disrespect for God and contempt for sincere but poor pilgrims.

Question 5

In Greek the word *zeal* is synonymous with *jealousy*. Jesus was jealous for his Father's reputation.

Question 8

In this statement Jesus is looking beyond the age of temple worship to the time when his body, offered up in sacrifice and raised in power, will be the new temple where God and humanity may meet face to face. Jesus is referring to himself as the actual living presence of God in their midst. This is no small claim.

The temple was the center of Jewish religion, representing the very presence of the living God. There was no more powerful symbol of God's presence than the temple. So in answer to their challenge that Jesus prove his authority to clear the temple, Jesus referred to himself as the temple (2:19, 21). He was the actual living presence of God in their midst. Later the disciples understood that he was referring to his sacrifice of himself, which would end the need for temple sacrifices. But at this time everyone though he was speaking about the massive temple structure, and they were dumbfounded.

Question 12

See also Jeremiah 7:1-19. Jesus' action was motivated not only by a zeal for his father's glory but also by a deep compassion for his people and the renewal of their worship. He no doubt hoped the "severe mercy" of his shocking correction would cause the priests to repent. Instead they demanded Jesus' proof of authorization through a miraculous sign rather than face Jesus' charge of having dishonored God.

SESSION TWO. JOHN 4:5-24.
Water for a Dry Soul.

Question 1

The sixth hour is about noon.

Question 3

The Jews had a strong prejudice against the Samaritans that had historical and religious roots. In 721 B.C. the Assyrians invaded the northern section of Israel and deported people living there. They left only a few poor Jews in the land. Then the Assyrians imported other conquered people and settled them in the former Jewish territory. The pagan Gentile population intermarried with the Jewish people and produced a mixed racial group called the Samaritans. Because of their mixed blood and mixed religion (their religion was a mixture of the Pentateuch, the first five books of the Bible, and pagan idolatry), the orthodox Jews viewed the Samaritans as worse than Gentiles. It was the accepted custom that Jews would not drink from the same vessel as Samaritans. Jewish food laws would have considered water in her jar contaminated

By asking for water, Jesus was intentionally crossing three cultural barriers. First, he spoke to a woman. Jewish men were instructed never to talk to any woman in public. Second, he spoke to an immoral woman who was living with a man she was not married to (v. 18). Third, he spoke to a Samaritan. But Jesus loved her and was willing to breach age-old conventions in order to reach her.

Question 4

This was a woman accustomed to being judged and condemned or used for immoral purposes. Based on the disciples' reaction to her, it must have been clear from her appearance what kind of woman she was. Her self-esteem had to be very low. So it is significant that Jesus treated her with dignity—asking her to meet his need for a drink. Jesus refused to see her as a despised Samaritan and instead related to her in authentic friendship and as a woman of worth.

Question 6

"Living water" is a vivid image in an arid land like Palestine. There are themes found in the Hebrew Bible that reference this, such as Ezekiel 36:25-27 and Jeremiah

2:13 and 17:13, where God himself is the "fountain of living water." And John 7:37-39 also sheds light by Jesus offering eternal life through the gift of the Spirit to all who believe in him.

Question 9

Jesus does not hesitate to be persuasive in order to reach her, but he refuses to manipulate her. He knows she needs to see the connection between her "thirst" and what Jesus is offering her. He sees her moral history, going from one man to the next, as a cry for fulfillment that only God can bring.

Question 10

Without allowing himself to be sidetracked, Jesus does not dismiss her question about worship. The fact that the Samaritans did not embrace anything other than the first five books of the Hebrew Bible limited their knowledge of God ("You worship that which you do not know," 4:22). Furthermore, it meant that they did not accept that God had directed David's decision to build the temple in Jerusalem. So Jesus corrects her concern for where one should worship by saying that true worshipers worship in spirit and truth. Jesus teaches throughout John's Gospel that he is the truth and he dispenses the Spirit to all who believe in him.

STUDY THREE. JOHN 6:1-35.
Soul Food.

Question 2

Jesus was testing Philip's faith so that it would grow.

Question 3

Philip thinks only in terms of the limited resources, not God's powerful resources—despite what he had just experienced during his succesful preaching tour. Jesus is never discouraged by what we have to offer no matter how meager. God delights in revealing his power through our weakness.

Question 7

The crowd, no doubt buoyed up in their nationalistic fervor as Passover celebration approaches, saw in Jesus the fulfillment of Deuteronomy 18:15-19. But Jesus rejects their attempts to set him up as a political leader to liberate them from Rome and departs abruptly. He also sends the disciples away, perhaps to protect them from the influence of this misguided zeal.

Question 8

Their main error is in being materialists. Their interest in Jesus lies in his ability to feed them.

Question 10

Jesus is trying to help them understand that the true food that satisfies our deepest needs is found in relationship with him.

STUDY FOUR. JOHN 9.
I Once Was Blind . . .

Question 1

The rabbis believed that there was no suffering without the cause being the sin of the person or the parents. Since he was blind from birth, this would have made his parents' suffering even more unbearable (although the rabbis believed it was even possible to sin in the womb). Not only did they have to cope with his disability but with the haunting shame of what might they have done wrong to bring about their son's blindness.

Jesus isn't teaching that the man and his parents are sinless, but rather that we can't assume a one-to-one relationship between our present problems and our sins of the past. Because sin came into our planet as a result of the fall in Genesis 3, we know that sometimes innocent people suffer and scoundrels get away with things they shouldn't. Regardless of the reasons for our suffering Jesus has the power to help us deal with it. Whether he chooses to heal us physically, or give us his grace and presence to bear our affliction, it can all bring glory to God.

Question 3

He would hear Jesus as he spat on the ground, he'd sense him stooping near him, he'd hear Jesus making a mud pie, he'd feel startled by the mud Jesus applies on his eyes and he'd hear Jesus' voice inches away telling him to go and wash the mud off.

Question 4

We don't know for sure. Perhaps Jesus was awakening faith in this man by involving him in a process that required a simple act of obedience.

Question 6

From the strictest Pharisaical standpoint, Jesus had broken their tradition (but not Scripture!) on at least two points. He healed on the Sabbath, which their tradition said was permissible only when life was in danger. And in making the mud he had kneaded on the Sabbath, which was considered work and thus forbidden. The "tradition of the elders" was a body of work that was written to interpret the Scripture. Unfortunately, the authors continually added more rules and laws until it became painfully minute in its demands, intolerably burdensome and often far from the original intent of Scripture.

Question 7

This should have been a time of great rejoicing, not only for their son's release from the bondage of blindness and begging, but for their release from shame and guilt. Instead they had to hide their joy and kowtow to the religious authorities for fear of being booted out of the temple.

Question 10

Jesus sought him out because he had been rejected from the temple. Jesus came to encourage him and also to lead him to faith. "Son of Man" was the title Jesus often used for himself. The reference here is to the figure of Daniel 7, which some Jews associated with the Messiah. What matters most is that Jesus is identifying himself as the one in whom the healed man should now believe.

Question 12

Jesus shows that the real sin wasn't the man's physical blindness (as the Pharisees assume) but the Pharisees' spiritual blindness that was caused by their stubbornness and hardness of heart. They refused to see their own sin and need for repentance.

Question 13

If time allows, you may want to go back and trace the key steps in the man's journey to faith. Note verses 7, 11-12, 15, 17, 25, 27, 30-33, 36-38.

STUDY FIVE. JOHN 11:1-44.
Eternal Life.

Question 2

Jesus had previously raised the daughter of Jairus from the dead and the son of the widow of Nain. But in retrospect some people may have decided they had simply been in a coma and that Jesus had only resuscitated them. In Lazarus' case it was unmistakably clear that he was dead, for his body was in the process of decay since it had been four days since his funeral; hence, Martha's concern that there would be an odor. Through this astonishing miracle Jesus is claiming to be the Lord of life and death for he showed his absolute authority even over decay and dissolution.

Question 4

Regarding the phrase "twelve hours of daylight" (11:9-10), Jesus is saying in a veiled way that it would not be so dangerous to go to Bethany. This is a use of double-entendre, referring not only to living in physical light or darkness. In the spiritual realm, because Jesus lives by the will of God, he is safe. As long as he followed

God's plan, no harm would come to him until the appointed time.

Question 5

We know him as "doubting Thomas," but there is something delightfully pragmatic about Thomas's character. He is willing to go to the mat for Jesus yet he still doesn't quite trust Jesus' decision to return to a dangerous place (as evidenced by his fatalistic statement).

Question 6

Martha clearly was eager to talk and be comforted by Jesus but she also may have slipped out so Jesus would not be endangered by any hostile Jews who were there to mourn her brother.

Question 8

Here Jesus juxtaposes two contradictory statements. He is saying, "In one sense believers physically die and are raised to life; in another sense, they do not die at all!" When Jesus claimed that those who believe in him should not die (11:26), he was not saying believers would never die physically. Rather, Jesus was declaring his ability to overcome spiritual death in our present life, and after physical death, to give everlasting life to those who put their trust in him (1 Cor 15:50-57).

Martha, like the Pharisees, believes that God will not leave faithful believers to pass into oblivion. Lazarus will rise when the messianic kingdom dawns at the general resurrection on the last day. "Martha believes in some such life at the distant horizon of history when the Messiah eventually appears. Jesus invites her to reshape her hope radically. Resurrection life which triumphs over death is not confined to the distant future, but is present here and now in him . . . to believe in Jesus means that death lies defeated (Bruce Milne, *The Message of John* [Downers Grove, Ill.: InterVarsity Press], p.163).

Question 9

Jesus knew what he was about to do, but he wept because he entered into the pain of Mary and Martha. Jesus demonstrated the compassion of God who hurts with us and for us. In Jesus' example we see that as his followers we need not fear death. However, this does not keep us from experiencing grief in the losses associated with death.

Question 10

It was never God's intention that death enter the human experience. Far more than sympathy for his friends' grief, Jesus feels rage at what Satan has introduced to the planet through tempting Adam and Eve and their subsequent disobedience. Romans 6:23 tells us that death came as a result of sin. It is death that is the object of Jesus' wrath, and behind death, the evil one who caused it to happen in the first place.

Question 11

In bringing Lazarus to life Jesus is demonstrating why he has come: to defeat Satan, to destroy death and to offer eternal life to those who place their trust in him. He will accomplish this ultimately through his death and resurrection. This miracle is also the clearest evidence to the deity of Jesus, and it shows that for those who believe, physical death is not the end—they live on.

Question 13

Jesus' love is not that of an indulgent parent who rushes to meet a child's every need. His delay in coming to Lazarus was a painful experience for Mary and Martha, yet it produced the fruit of deeper faith and trust in God. Jesus' actions didn't make them happy in the moment, but they ultimately produced greater holiness and deeper faith.

STUDY SIX. JOHN 19:1-37.
Death Isn't the Last Word.

Question 1

Pilate was clearly impressed by Jesus—his calm, dignified manner, the confidence with which he makes his claims, and he had no doubt heard about Jesus' signs and wonders. Pilate was probably also affected by a message from his wife warning him that Jesus was innocent and that he should leave him alone because she had had a nightmare about Jesus (Mt 27:19). Pilate was probably a superstitious pagan and dreams were highly significant to Romans at that time. Even if they no longer believed in the Greek and Roman deities, they would have a terrible dread of acting contrary to guidance in a dream.

Question 2

Pilate clearly believes that Jesus is innocent (Jn 18:38), and he knew that flogging before sentencing for guilt was illegal under Roman law. But Pilate's previous attempts to free Jesus have failed, so perhaps he is trying a different tack—having Jesus flogged, presumably in the hope that this lesser punishment will appease his accusers.

The flogging practices in those days were brutal. The victim usually had his upper body bare and his hands tied to a pillar. Up to forty lashes were permitted with a three-pronged metal-tipped rope, which would have left Jesus with deep gashes of raw skin.

Not only did Jesus endure the physical trauma of the flogging, but he was mocked and ridiculed as well (Mt 27; Mk 15; Lk 23). Perhaps Pilate brings Jesus out to the crowd, mockingly dressed as a king and clearly suffering physical agonies (the thorns of his crown were comprised of jagged spikes of up to twelve inches in length that had been rammed into his head), to elicit pity and to show how insignificant their case against Jesus was. Pilate underestimated their determination to see Jesus killed.

Question 3

Pilate was alarmed by these references to Jesus' divine claims. He wants to be sure that this Jesus wasn't some "supernatural" visitor who would come back to haunt him.

Question 6

They unequivocally charged treason—that Jesus intended to usurp the authority of Caesar. If Pilate does not put him to death, he becomes implicated in Jesus' crime. And the Jewish priests will make sure Caesar

Tiberius himself hears about it! Palestine had become so difficult to rule that it was regarded as a dreaded post. Furthermore Pilate had already done several extremely insensitive things in Judea that outraged the Jews. He could not afford to let one more complaint reach Caesar.

Nothing is more sacred to the Jewish covenant than the kingship of God. The statement in verse 15, "We have no king but Caesar," is true blasphemy—the very thing they are accusing Jesus of!

Question 7

Physically, Jesus would have been very weak, having already lost a good deal of blood, having been repeatedly struck in the face and having not slept for thirty-six hours. He was under great strain, and he was no doubt contemplating what he was about to endure on the cross—not just physically but most of all spiritually.

Question 8

The three main languages of the day were Greek, Latin and Hebrew (Aramaic was a derivative of Hebrew), and they are all used on the sign.

Perhaps Pilate wanted everyone to know his contempt for what the Jewish leaders had done. Sadly, when it's too late to make a difference, Pilate is implacable about changing the title.

Question 12

First, the crucifixion was a horrendous method of capitol punishment. It was a slow, long agonizing death that ended finally by suffocation. So horrific was the suffering that no Roman was permitted to undergo it, however heinous the crime.

At death the blood and serum separate. There can be no question that Jesus was truly dead. He had not fainted only to be resuscitated in the grave as some posit.

Question 13

John tells us that Jesus' final triumphant cry is "It is finished." The Greek meaning is closer to "It is accomplished." The task for which he came has been completed—the whole plan of salvation is accomplished. Furthermore, John wants us to know that Jesus chose the moment of his death. In John 19:30, we are told that Jesus shouted, "It is finished." That would have been impossible in the usual crucifixion. The victim would lose so much blood that he would retain insufficient oxygen even to continue breathing. He would have been incapable of more than a whisper. Jesus said, "No one takes [my life] from me, but I lay it down of my own accord" (Jn 10:18).

STUDY 7. JOHN 20.
The End of Doubt.

Question 1

Mary of Magdala was the first to see Jesus after his resurrection. Previously, he had cast seven demons out of Mary (Lk 8:2-3). She was among the women who attended the Lord and disciples during their Galilean ministry, providing for them out of their means (Mk 15:41).

Question 2

Peter and John ran to the grave to check Mary's story. John, being considerably younger than Peter, arrives ahead. When he peers inside he sees the linen shroud but not the body! John waits for Peter before he goes inside; perhaps out of respect, for Peter had been his father's senior partner in their fishing business, and Peter had been the leader, under Jesus, of their team. Furthermore, John's nature was reflective and intense, not impulsive like Peter's.

Question 3

The position of the burial wrapping (vv. 6-7) is significant. First, if Jesus' body had been stolen, then the robbers wouldn't have taken the time to so carefully rewrap the linens; they would have been in too much of a hurry. Jewish burial practice involved wrapping the body in strips of linen from the shoulders to the toes. As the wrapping was done, a mixture of gummy spices was spread on the cloth to hold the binding. A large square of linen was wrapped over the head and was tied under the jaw.

What Peter and John saw when they investigated was that the linen burial cocoon was still in place, but the body was gone. Jesus had exited the shroud while leaving it nearly intact! The disciples knew that something supernatural had taken place ("John believed"), but they didn't understand he had resurrected, as evidenced by their shock at seeing him in verse 9. They may have thought he had become a ghost in order to be able to exit the heavy shroud. Or perhaps they believed God had taken him.

Question 5

There could be several reasons. For one, Mary is distraught and weeping, and she never imagined she would see Jesus again. But Jesus had not been resuscitated like her brother Lazarus. He had passed through death and was now part of a new order. His appearing "different" in some indefinable way is to be expected.

Question 6

The moment of recognition is portrayed beautifully (v. 16). The one word Jesus spoke that totally transformed her life forever was her own name, "Mary." Jesus said, "My sheep know my voice." The Lord deals with each one of us intimately; he knows our name.

Question 7

"Don't touch me" There are several ways these words could be interpreted. First, Jesus is not objecting to Mary touching him. Rather he could be saying, "You don't need to cling to me because you will see me again, and it's urgent that you go and tell the brokenhearted disciples that you have seen me and I am alive." Or, alternatively, because Jesus will be ascending to heaven soon, Mary will have to learn a new kind of relationship with Jesus, not through touch but through faith and through the Holy Spirit.

Question 8

She was the first believer who actually saw Jesus alive and spoke to him and touched him. In Jewish culture at that time, a woman would not have been considered a valid witness. Jesus is elevating the role and importance of women by allowing Mary this place of honor and significance.

Question 9

The Hebrew word for "peace" is *shalom* and has deep meaning in Hebrew. It encompasses a sense of well-being in its fullest sense. It gathers up all the blessings of the kingdom of God. On a practical note, the disciples also needed peace in light of their terror at seeing Jesus.

Question 12

Jesus was always with them, as much when they couldn't see him as when they could! This was one of the reasons for the termination of his appearances, to rely instead on his presence with them through his Holy Spirit.

Questions 15-16

You may need to choose between these questions if time is running short.

Question 16

The Jewish leaders and the Roman government turned Jerusalem upside down to find his corpse. That was all they needed to prove it was a hoax. Yet his body was never discovered. Instead over a forty-day period, Jesus appeared in bodily form to more than five hundred people. Without the physical resurrection of Jesus, Christianity would collapse like a deck of cards! The apostle Paul declared in his letter to the Corinthian believers, "If Christ has not been raised, our preaching is useless and so is your faith" (1 Cor 15:14). Why? Because biblical, authentic Christianity can be experienced only through a personal relationship with the living Lord Jesus Christ.

Other books by Rebecca Manley Pippert

Hope Has Its Reasons

This is a book geared for people who want honest answers to honest questions. The author examines the persistent human longings that all of us share about significance, meaning, life and truth, and the search for security. Only after she unravels the core of the real problem that plagues us does she explore how Christ can meet our longings and solve our human crisis. There are no canned formulas or saccharine clichés. Realism rings in the stories she tells and the ideas she pursues. In doing so she leads us beyond the search for our own significance to the reasons for our hope in discovering God. *197 pp., 2278-X*

A Heart for God

How can God use the difficulties and sufferings in our lives to build character and deepen our faith? The biblical character David faced some desperate circumstances and some tough choices. So do we, day by day. The author shows us how God is able to use the everyday grit and glory of our lives to shape a holy life within us. Using David as her guide she helps us understand the way Christian virtue is developed in our souls and vices are rooted out. We learn how we, like David, can choose the good, overcome temptation and grow to be one who has a heart for God. *236 pp., 2341-7*

Transformation

Would you like to move from despair to hope? Would you like to transform your feelings of fear to faith? Would you like to turn envy into compassion? The Bible shows how David turned these negative emotions in his life into godly character qualities. In this Christian Basics Bible Study, based on the Bible's account of David and the book *A Heart for God,* you'll investigate David's life, choices, mistakes and triumphs. Then you'll discover how you can make the same transformation in your own life. *6 studies, 2019-1*